IMAGES
of America

LOVELAND

IMAGES
of America

LOVELAND

Laurel Benson and Debra Benson Faulkner

ARCADIA
PUBLISHING

Published by Arcadia Publishing
Charleston, South Carolina

Printed in the United States of America

Library of Congress Control Number: 2012939800

For all general information, please contact Arcadia Publishing:
Telephone 843-853-2070
Fax 843-853-0044
E-mail sales@arcadiapublishing.com
For customer service and orders:
Toll-Free 1-888-313-2665

Visit us on the Internet at www.arcadiapublishing.com

*To husband and father Donald Benson, who
chose Loveland as our home.*

CONTENTS

ACKNOWLEDGMENTS

The most rewarding part of a book project like this one is the chance to collaborate with people willing to share their information and insights. We owe a great debt to Jennifer Cousino, history curator for the Loveland Museum/Gallery. There would have been no book without her. She generously opened the photograph collection of the museum and arranged for the digitization of pile upon pile of the images we selected. She always found answers to our questions and did it all with a smile.

Sue Osborn, a descendant of pioneer William Osborn, brought forth family pictures and anecdotes, as did Susan Jessup and Dave Armstrong of Sylvan Dale Ranch. Jim Worthen of the Loveland Chamber of Commerce was a font of information on local business history. Edna Walters of Sunny Jim's Candy Farm and Chauncey Taylor of Johnson's Corner shared photographs and stories of those landmark Loveland businesses. Developer Chad McWhinney related the history of his family in the area and shared his vision of the community's future.

Rick Savino explained the origins of the Stone Age Fair, and Coi Drummond Gehrig provided images from the Denver Public Library's amazing western history collection. "Dr. Colorado" Tom Noel graciously supplied photographs from his extensive private collection. Chuck Yungkurth of the Colorado Railroad Museum came through for us with an image of the right kind of engine from the right period of history. GeoEye's Kerri Rose zeroed in on an image of the HP campus from space with astonishing efficiency.

Dixie Huff and others on the staff of the Loveland Library went the extra mile to dig out information for us. Additional facts and stories came from Gloria Grotzinger, Jan Hemberger, Juanita Cisneros, George Walbye, and Fred Fishburn.

We wish to express special thanks to Tom Benson and James Faulkner for providing technical assistance to the computer-challenged authors with infinite patience. Local historian and author Ken Jessen not only supplied photographs of Hewlett Packard's early Loveland years, but also graciously reviewed our manuscript for accuracy. Every time we asked for information or answers, it was given enthusiastically. Working with and getting to know these Lovelanders made this book a labor of love.

INTRODUCTION

The community of Loveland, Colorado, has redefined itself many times since its inception. From supplying fur traders and prospectors to embracing sculptors and public artists, this Front Range enclave has reshaped its role and reinvented its identity time and time again. Each "rebranding" has left its mark on the city as it exists today, enfolding earlier incarnations into the ever-changing fabric of Loveland's municipal tapestry.

The story began with a Mexican mountain man, Mariano Medina, who capitalized on Colorado's 1859 gold rush by establishing a trading post and toll bridge just downstream from the mouth of Big Thompson Canyon near present-day Loveland. Mariano's Crossing equipped hopeful gold seekers with necessities, including food produced by the area's earliest homesteaders. Farmers harvested grass hay and found that crops like barley, wheat, and corn grew well along the Front Range. Early irrigation ditches brought essential water from the Big Thompson River to outlying farms. Ranchers, too, staked claims in the river valley, raising cattle on the open range to provide beef for settlers and stagecoach travelers along the Overland Trail.

The pioneer hamlets of Winona and St. Louis sprouted along the river as a stage stop and flour-milling center, respectively. The two merged to share the services of a blacksmith, a doctor, a hotel, a general store, and the Big Thompson post office. But like the rest of the territory, the little community struggled with isolation and the associated high costs of freight and travel.

It was the arrival of the Colorado Central Railroad (CCRR) that literally put the fledgling community on the map. Named for the CCRR's founder, W.A.H. Loveland, the town was founded in 1877 and was well positioned to boom as a farming and rail center. Loveland prospered with agriculture-related industries, including flour milling and canning.

Pioneering women, as well as men, helped to shape and improve the town. Loveland ladies, be they professionals or public officials, teachers or librarians, all contributed to the town's development. Some owned businesses, while others managed farms and ranches. They supported churches and charities and campaigned for cultural improvements, making the community a better place on many levels.

Local irrigation systems and rail access were key factors in Great Western (GW) Sugar Company's decision to open its first factory in Loveland in 1901. The sugar beet industry dominated the town's economy for the next 60 years, employing both field laborers and processing professionals. Cherry orchards also flourished in the area, providing seasonal work for pickers. Loveland cherry pies and cherry cider gained a reputation for excellence among locals and tourists.

In the late 1800s, only the most intrepid adventure travelers ventured into the mountains outside Loveland. But the construction of a primitive road through Big Thompson Canyon in 1904–1905 opened the way for tourists from Loveland to Estes Park. With the dawn of the automobile age and the 1915 designation of Rocky Mountain National Park, Loveland became the "Gateway to the Rockies" for early motorists. The 1935 construction of Highway 34 made the route more accessible, and tourist-attracting businesses set up shop along the highway between Loveland and the canyon mouth.

The creation of Lake Loveland in 1932 provided not only a much-needed reservoir for local agriculture, but also a scenic and recreational attraction around which the town continued to grow. The Bureau of Reclamation's massive Grand Lake–Big Thompson water diversion project was headquartered in Loveland in the 1940s. The ambitious undertaking brought water from the Western Slope through a tunnel blasted under the Continental Divide. The project created a series of dams and reservoirs that still provide both water and hydroelectric power to the region.

During the early 1950s, Loveland's postmaster, Elmer Ivers, decided to promote the aptly named community as the "Sweetheart City." His valentine re-mailing program encouraged people from all around the country to send their cards with the romantic postmark. In addition, an annual Cowboy Cupid cachet with poem was hand-stamped onto each envelope. It was not long before the local brouhaha came to include the selection of a young Cowboy Cupid and Miss Loveland Valentine as chamber of commerce ambassadors for the re-mailing campaign. The annual emphasis on postal romance defined the town as a warm-hearted—albeit a bit corny—place.

Despite such determined boosterism, by the late 1950s, Loveland's economy was in a funk. With the acquisition and development of a new industrial park, local business leaders succeeded in enticing emerging electronics giant Hewlett Packard (HP) to expand its Silicon Valley operations into Colorado. HP took to the location and soon built one of its first major manufacturing plants in Big Thompson Business Park. By the 1970s, the company had surpassed GW as Loveland's biggest employer. Other high-tech and light industrial firms, including Samsonite's Lego and Woodward Governor, followed HP's lead, creating jobs and spawning unprecedented community growth.

As Coloradans prepared to celebrate 100 years of statehood in 1976, Loveland found itself at the center of the greatest natural disaster in the state's history. Torrential rains on Estes Park and the upper reaches of Big Thompson sent a devastating wall of water rushing down the steep and narrow canyon. The loss of life and property in the tragedy was staggering, reminding residents that nature was ultimately untamable and casting a pall over the centennial celebrations.

Loveland's latest cachet began with its first invitational sculpture show and sale in 1991. One local art-casting foundry led to several, and renowned artists gravitated to the supportive and inspiring location. The community gradually earned its current reputation as an international sculpture capital. Loveland's public art program, supported by a local sales tax, is one of the first and most extensive in the nation, responsible for embellishing everything from parks to electrical transformers and enhancing the quality of life.

Loveland's proximity to the mountains, coupled with its family- and arts-friendly ambiance, continues to characterize this thriving municipality. In recent decades, the former small town has sprawled so that old-timers hardly recognize the place. Along the northbound arteries, it is sometimes difficult to tell where Loveland ends and Fort Collins begins. To the east, with the opening of the Centerra Shopping Complex and the Budweiser Events Center, Loveland spills across Interstate 25. In the 21st century, Loveland is, to a greater or lesser extent, all the things it has been before and much, much more.

Unless otherwise noted, all images in this book are included courtesy of the Loveland Museum/ Gallery. This take on Loveland's history is by no means comprehensive. The story told herein was shaped to a large extent by the images available. It offers but a sampling; a scrapbook of people, places, events, and developments that have defined this sweetheart of a spot over the years.

One

TRADING PLACE

Long before the first white settlers—even long before the Indians—there was the river. Because of the Big Thompson River, Loveland is where it is and, to a great extent, what it is. (Courtesy of S. Jessup)

Native Americans claim to have inhabited the area "forever." The nomadic Arapaho frequently camped along the river, where there was plentiful grass for their horses and a good supply of fish and game. Taking advantage of the relatively mild Front Range climate, generations of Indians wintered here. (Courtesy of T. Noel.)

The Cheyenne, too, followed the river, finding it the perfect place for hunting, providing them with food and hides. In the early 1800s, fur trappers and mountain men were drawn to the river. As early as 1810, David Thompson, an English engineer and astronomer, explored the area, leaving his name on the river and the valley.

Evidence of the Indians' presence is found in the many stone arrowheads uncovered in the area. Archeologists, both professional and amateur, gather annually at the Stone Age Fair in Loveland to share their finds. Harold M. Dunning was instrumental in attracting the fair to Loveland in 1940. Sponsored by the Loveland Archeological Society, its proceeds fund scholarships for Colorado State University and University of Wyoming archaeological students. (Author's collection.)

Mexican mountain man Mariano Modena was the first recorded permanent settler in the area, in 1858. He lived peacefully with the Indians, carrying on a trading relationship benefitting both parties. Mariano's Indian wife was called, variously, Tacanecy, Marie, or John. According to legend, the colorful Medina's last wish was to be buried with his favorite horse, wagon, and a keg of whiskey to accompany him into the afterlife. (Courtesy of T. Noel.)

Medina built a toll bridge across the Big Thompson River and fenced his land so that travelers were forced to use it. It was a plank bridge, wide enough for a wagon and team. Medina's usual $1 toll tended to increase arbitrarily during periods of high water. His fellow Mexicans, however, never had to pay.

Because of the bridge, Medina's settlement was commonly called Mariano's Crossing. In 1868, John Washburn, the postmaster, suggested the name Namaqua and by 1860, the settlement consisted of 45 families in 22 houses, a store, a saloon, a stable, lodging for travelers, and a stone fort with 20-inch-thick walls and six gun ports. Generals Grant, Sheridan, and Sherman, as well as Kit Carson, visited the spot at various times.

In 1862, Mariano's Crossing became a stop on the Overland Trail. The stage road came down from the bluffs where Derby Hill is now and followed approximately the route that became the railroad. From there, it went north to La Porte and even farther to Virginia Dale and Laramie. Stage stops provided lodging and food for weary passengers and fresh horses for the journey onwards.

Most early settlers in the area were lured by natural resources other than gold. In the sea of hardy prairie grasses that surrounded them, they had something the mountain towns could use. Prospectors needed feed for their horses and mules, and the hungry critters ate native grass as readily as they did cultivated hay. Mining camp residents were willing to pay handsomely for the harvests of foothills farms.

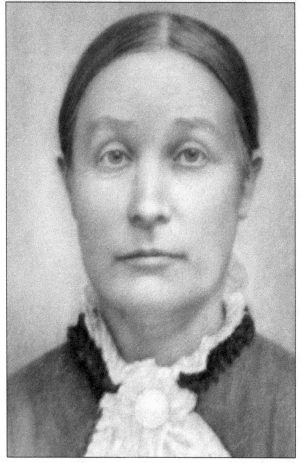

The Washburn home was among the earliest in the area. John Washburn, the first county judge, and his wife, Albina, were very active in the budding settlement, and their home operated as an Overland Stage station for several years. An 1862 route change necessitated by Indian uprisings brought the line through Larimer County. "Home stations" like theirs were positioned every 50 miles, supplying fresh drivers and horses and offering hot meals for travelers.

Albina Washburn was known as "Mother Washburn" to stage travelers. She was the first schoolteacher in the area, conducting three-month school terms in their log cabin for local children of all ages. The Washburns were postmasters for the early Big Thompson post office. Their daughter, Winona, often delivered the mail to outlying homesteads on horseback, and the little community that grew up along the river around the Washburn house was named for her.

Most early settlers homesteaded along the Big Thompson River, but when those prime locations were taken, others who staked their claims farther away from the water source built irrigation ditches to channel water to their land. In 1861, the Big Thompson Ditch Company filed on 96.5 feet of water from the river. H.B. Chubbuck dug the first ditch, pictured here, now known as the English Ditch.

A steady supply of water and decent soil encouraged settlers to cultivate a variety of crops. Oats, beans, wheat, potatoes, and barley were raised on many farms, along with livestock. Despite producing more than they could consume, the pioneers lacked an efficient form of transportation for distribution to make their ventures profitable.

William and Margaret Osborn were also among the earliest settlers, establishing their farm in 1860. When William traded his claim in the town of Gold Dust for farmland, he was assured it would be easy to locate. There were only two trees in the area, and the one to the north marked the corner of his property. With money from the sale of her garden produce, Margaret Osborn purchased the first cereal seed brought into the area.

An Osborn Farm tradition involved tossing a man's hat out into the barley field to gauge the crop's progress. When the hat sat atop the grain, it was ready to harvest. (Courtesy of S. Osborn.)

The Cheyenne and Arapaho tribes were still in the area when early pioneers came to settle. A huge cottonwood on the Osborn's property became known as the Indian Tree because Black Kettle, an Arapaho chief, often camped briefly with his band and roasted antelope and other game at the foot of the old tree. It is not recorded whether he ever shared his bounty. The ancient tree's toppling symbolized the end of one era and the beginning of another. (Courtesy of S. Osborn.)

The principal occupation of many early settlers was harvesting prairie grass for hay in the fall and winter. Hauled up to mountain mining towns such as Central City, it fed the many horses, mules, and burros so crucial to prospecting operations. The harvesters charged $75–$150 per ton, which they then used to purchase supplies. A typical round-trip trade journey to the mining camps took nine days by ox team.

17

The settlement of St. Louis owed its name to a bag of flour. Andrew Douty's gristmill struggled because consumers preferred flour ground in St. Louis, Missouri. In a stroke of inspiration, Douty printed his flour sacks with "4X Flour, Made in St. Louis" and under that, in tiny letters, "Colorado" or "Made in Big Thompson." His business boomed, and soon the whole area adopted the name. (Courtesy of Loveland Chamber of Commerce.)

A few miles downriver from Namaqua, several businesses arose in the fledgling settlement of Winona, including a hotel to accommodate travelers. After the success of the Douty Mill, this hotel was named for St. Louis, as was the mill's flour.

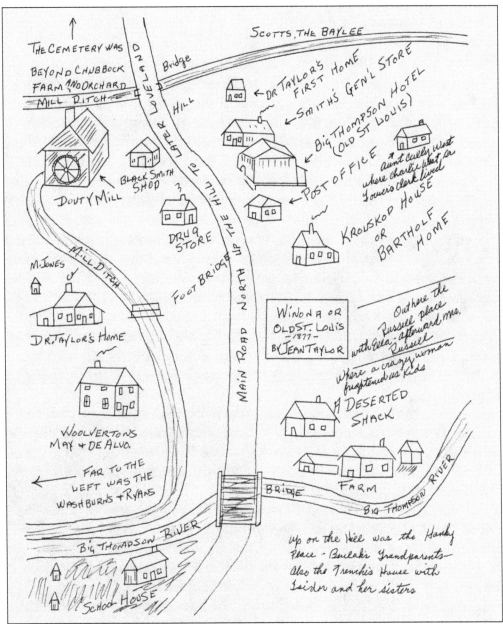

The following text appears within the hand-drawn map:

SCOTTS, THE BAYLEE

THE CEMETERY WAS BEYOND CHUBBOCK FARM AND ORCHARD
MILL DITCH

Bridge
LATER LOVELAND
Hill

← DR TAYLOR'S FIRST HOME
← SMITH'S GEN'L STORE
BIG THOMPSON HOTEL (OLD ST LOUIS)

POST OFFICE
Aunt cally West where charlie West jr Lower's clerk lived

KROUSKOP HOUSE OR BARTHOLF HOME

DOUTY MILL
BLACK SMITH SHOP

M. JONES
MILL DITCH
Foot Bridge up the Hill to

DRUG STORE

DR. TAYLOR'S HOME

WOOLVERTONS MAY & DE ALVO.

FAR TO THE LEFT WAS THE WASHBURNS & RYANS

MAIN ROAD NORTH UP THE HILL

WINONA OR OLD ST. LOUIS -1877- BY JEAN TAYLOR

Out here the Russell place with Eela - afterward mrs. Russell

Where a crazy woman frightened us kids

A DESERTED SHACK

FARM

BIG THOMPSON RIVER

BRIDGE

BIG THOMPSON RIVER

SCHOOL HOUSE

up on the hill was the Hanky Place - Beulah's Grandparents - Also the Frenchie's House with Leida and her sisters

Jean Taylor (later Gower) drew this map of her hometown, variously known as St. Louis, Winona, and Big Thompson. In reminiscences with local historian Harold M. Dunning, she recalled details like the way the waterwheel spray at Douty's Mill created rainbows on sunny days. Taylor's father was the community's first doctor, who also served as a druggist and ran a makeshift hospital in their home. Winona became known as a place where those suffering from respiratory ailments might breathe easier in the high, thin, dry air. The little settlement already had a school and a post office in 1877. Above the farm on the lower right, the "Deserted Shack" is where Taylor says "a crazy woman frightened us kids."

In 1860, one of the area's first pioneers, John Hahn, began raising cattle on 480 acres, but soon expanded his operation. Through his daughter Jessie's marriage to Clyde C. McWhinney, Hahn acquired even more property, becoming one of the largest livestock dealers in Larimer County. In 1897, Hahn erected an impressive brick residence on the corner of West and Third Streets, considered the finest in town. (Courtesy of C. McWhinney.)

Hardworking cowboys like (from left to right) Lee Hays, James Cross, and Alex Hornickle rarely had the time to pose for photographs. Each season, they drove Hays's cattle herd hundreds of miles from their spread to market in Riverton, Wyoming. In the 1860s and 1870s, the Loveland area struggled with isolation and the associated high freight costs. Without reliable connections to supply hubs and the outside world, the hopeful homesteaders fought an uphill battle.

Two

RAILROAD STOP

In 1877, the Colorado Central Railroad chugged slowly northward, straight through David Barnes's farmland, totally ignoring Namaqua and St. Louis to the west and east. And that made all the difference. Rail access was nearly as essential as water to success in the American West, and business and development followed the tracks. This Colorado Central engine, built by the Schenectaty Locomotive Company, was photographed in 1885. (Courtesy of Colorado Railroad Museum.)

On an insider tip from his friend W.A.H. Loveland, David Barnes snapped up 320 acres on "The Bluff" above the Big Thompson in 1871. He dug one of the first irrigation ditches in the area, the only landmark that still bears his name. After initial years of struggles with grasshopper devastation to his wheat crops, Barnes was suddenly sitting pretty because the railroad platted a new town on his property, greatly increasing its value.

The modest Barnes shrugged off the suggestion that the new town be named Barnesville and instead chose to honor his friend, William Austin Hamilton Loveland, president of the Colorado Central Railroad. Loveland, a soldier, statesman, educator, and newspaper man, most likely never set foot in his namesake community. (Courtesy of T. Noel.)

A tent served as the first depot for the Colorado Central in Loveland. A brick depot, located west of the main line, was built in 1877. In 1902, the Colorado and Southern Railroad constructed a depot east of the tracks (above). The second depot featured a comfortable waiting room for passengers so that they no longer had to share space with freight, which often included an animal or two. This eastside depot also eliminated the problem of stopped trains blocking Fourth Street. A 47,500-gallon water tower refreshed the steam locomotives of both railroads with water delivered by the English Ditch.

Anxious to be first on the scene, John Herzinger and Samuel Harter camped all night on the town site of Loveland on October 10, 1877. Bright and early the next morning, they purchased the first three lots from David Barnes. By 1878, Herzinger and Harter had constructed this two-story brick building on the lots for the princely sum of $4,500. Known as the H&H Store building, it still stands today.

The Exchange Hotel, the Loveland Hotel, and the Big Thompson Hotel accommodated early train travelers on Fourth Street, which soon became the main street of town. When the Loveland Hotel burned down, it was rebuilt as the much larger Lovelander Hotel.

The Reporter, founded in 1880, was the first newspaper in Loveland, publishing local news for the next 10 years, despite multiple owners and multiple location changes. Later, *The Loveland Leader*, *The Register*, and *The Herald* all competed on the reporting scene at intervals. Finally, in 1922, the *Reporter-Herald* emerged as the one newspaper for Loveland.

The Osborn, Ferguson, and Co. Hardware and Implements Store was another early Loveland business. Over the years, the partnerships changed, but a Ferguson was always in the mix. Ferguson Hardware store was the longest continually owned family business in town until the 1980s.

Charles H. Wheeler built a flourmill in 1880, calling it the Centennial Mill. When it burned to the ground, a second mill replaced it and, 11 years later, new owners redubbed it the Loveland Farmers Milling and Elevator Company, the first of seven subsequent name changes culminating with Loveland Feed and Grain, which it has remained since 1968. In its heyday, the mill produced 125 sacks of flour per day.

Blacksmiths kept horses shod and wagons repaired in every community. R.R. George Washington Rogers, one of the few black men in the area, was the first smithy in Winona/St. Louis. He later abandoned the trade to become a barber. Succeeding Rogers as early Loveland blacksmiths were Bert Davis in 1884 and Chet Apgas in 1906.

Iron horses did not supplant the four-legged kind as the main mode of transportation in the area. Covered wagons like this one were common sights in the early days on Fourth Street.

George Foote and Virgil Stoddard ran a flourishing business with their Livery, Feed, and Sale Stable in the early 1880s. Their establishment, one of the most important in town, was on the corner of Fourth Street and Cleveland Avenue. As a lucrative sideline, Foote & Stoddard shuttled tourists from the Loveland depot over Bald Mountain to Estes Park. The harrowing trip took four and a half hours, barring any catastrophes.

Fire was a constant worry in early Loveland, where frame buildings, dry climate, and kerosene lamps made for a volatile combination. In 1883, hose companies like Barthold Hose Company were composed of stalwart men in harness, pulling a large wheeled cart containing the rolled-up

water hose. In addition to river or ditch water, a cistern 10 feet in diameter at the corner of Fourth Street and Cleveland Avenue could be tapped in case of fire.

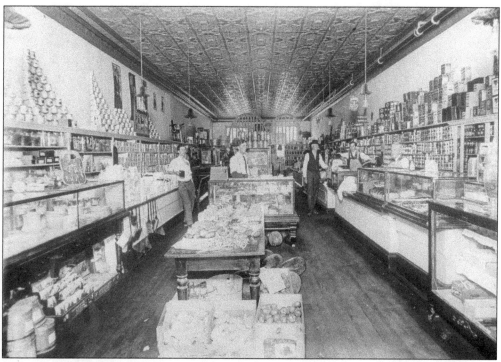

A grocery store supplemented the food folks raised themselves. Grocers Krenz and Orr sold goods that could not be found locally, as well as dishes and household tools. Bakeries, shoe stores, clothing stores, bookstores, restaurants, and drugstores also sprouted along Fourth Street, while a cigar store, a billiard parlor, and a saloon catered to the gentlemen.

These downtown Loveland businessmen were purveyors of tires and parts for bicycles, a tremendously popular recreational contraption around 1900. Women in particular relished the freedom and independence the two-wheeled transporters made possible.

The "Maggie Murphy Potato" appeared in this 1895 *Loveland Reporter* photograph, reportedly weighing 86 pounds, 10 ounces. J.B. Swan swore he had grown it. The photograph was so astonishing that it was featured in "Ripley's Believe It or Not!" Eventually, W.L. Thorndyke, the newspaper editor, admitted it had been a hoax, to the embarrassment of many and the amusement of others. The "potato" was actually made of wood.

Alfred Wild bought 640 acres near the Devil's Backbone in 1880. In 1885, he discovered gypsum on his property and two years later, he constructed a mill to process the soft mineral for use in plaster, drywall, and fertilizer. Wild's mill operated until 1915, when it was sold to U.S. Gypsum. Wild's large home, called Peep O' Day, later became a bed-and-breakfast known as Wild Lane Inn, operated by Alfred's grandson.

31

The Corn Roast Festival began in 1894 as Loveland's first all-community celebration. Lasting three days, it began with a parade with a band and floats. A free dinner, horse races, balloon ascensions, carnival rides, band concerts, theater productions, and bombastic speeches drew enthusiastic crowds. The highlight of the 1904 festival was the widely advertised badger fight. Many people eagerly awaited the fight, but the Denver Humane Society was horrified. They charged up to Loveland to stop it, accompanied by renowned muckraking reporter Nelly Bly, only to find the whole thing was a joke. Today's Corn Roast Festival includes booths for refreshments and crafts, team corn husking, and corn eating competitions. Much of the festival is as it once was, but fortunately sans the speeches.

David Barnes generously donated corner lots for churches and hauled in two loads of cottonwood trees to enhance the landscaping. Institutions like churches and schools set Loveland apart from the more raucous and uncivilized mining boomtowns in the mountains. The Methodist church was first in the area in 1866, followed by the Presbyterian church in 1875, the Catholic church in 1877, the Baptist church in 1878, and the Christian church, shown here, in 1879.

Schools grew up alongside families, meeting in storerooms or basements early on. East Side School (later Washington School) was built on Third Street in 1881. This photograph was taken from the bell tower on the roof of the first two-story school building. With all the open space surrounding it, there was plenty of room for a playground. Sarah Milner was hired as the first public school teacher in the area.

Posed here on the steps of Lincoln School are teachers, from left to right, (first row) Carrie Martin, Esther Bailey, Mary Blair, and Adah Ellis; (second row) Ethel Clampit, Eunice Mosley, Maud Harrison, and Harriet Tuggy. When Lincoln was built in 1907, care was taken to preserve the elm tree in the yard, known as the Washington Elm, an offshoot of the tree under which George Washington took charge of his troops.

Loveland's Eliza Johnson made national news in 1891 when she became the first woman elected to public office in the United States, as president of the local school board. For many years, Johnson proctored the county teachers' examinations and spearheaded the local Women's Christian Temperance Union. The Daughters of the American Revolution planted a tree in her memory in Lakeside Park, established on land given to the city by her husband, Thomas Johnson.

Several music organizations struck up in the 1880s. The Cornet Band began in 1881 and became the Loveland Military Band in 1889. They gave concerts in the West Side Park bandstand. A drum corps was started in 1883 and a community chorus in 1888. Four years earlier, the A&B Opera House, named for financiers E.I. Allen and Frank Barthold, presented its first Loveland performance: *Uncle Tom's Cabin*.

The Loveland Woman's Club was organized in 1903, as was the Women's Current Events Club. Winning the vote in 1893, a full 27 years before national women's suffrage, Colorado women wielded considerable clout. During the Progressive Era of the early 20th century, determined Loveland ladies set about "Municipal Housekeeping," cleaning up and culturally uplifting the community. Among other things, they successfully campaigned for public parks and a lending library.

Train engines like this miniature replica steam locomotive still thrill in Loveland. The train has chugged around North Lake Park each summer since 1976, driven by members of the Lion's Club. Children blowing its whistle scatter the geese. Though it may be impossible for children today to imagine the railroad as anything more than a novelty, it became increasingly important to Loveland in the early 1900s.

Three

SUGAR BEET TOWN

LOVELAND SUGAR BEET FACTORY.   LOVELAND, COLO.

Great Western (GW) Sugar Company's first sugar beet factory gave a huge boost to Loveland's economy. The flagship facility was dedicated on November 21, 1901, before a cheering crowd of 3,000—at a time when the total population of Loveland was just 2,500. The community raised a substantial amount of money to subsidize the plant's construction. For the next six decades, GW was the town's largest industry.

CHAS. BOETTCHER

German immigrant Charles Boettcher made his first million selling hardware to prospectors during the Leadville silver boom of the late 1870s. Unlike many Colorado millionaires who sank all their money into mining ventures, the business-savvy Boettcher understood the wisdom of diversification. Besides investing in livestock, packing plants, railroads, utilities, and concrete, he founded the Great Western Sugar Company, an enterprise that soon provided an economic infusion to Colorado. (Courtesy of T. Noel.)

Analyses done by the State Agricultural College showed that the soil and climate conditions around Loveland were ideal for nurturing sugar beets. The ugly tubers were planted in April or May and took about 190 days to mature. In the final months of growth, the beets, which weighed an average of five pounds each, needed lots of water to produce the highest sugar content.

An extremely labor-intensive crop, sugar beets provided jobs for many unskilled workers. Initially, Russian-German immigrants, the *Volga Deutsch*, supplied most of the "stoop labor"—hoeing, planting, weeding, thinning, and topping the beets. They were joined by Japanese immigrants in the early decades of the 20th century. By the 1920s, Mexicans made up the majority of sugar beet field hands. Sugar beet fieldwork was backbreaking. Whole families toiled together in the fields, even young children. Only those too little to stand or walk stayed home, usually unattended. The hardest working field hands sometimes got the opportunity to move up to supervisor and possibly even to small landowner.

A BEET DUMP NEAR LOVELAND, COLO.

Key to Great Western's success was Boettcher's ownership of other businesses utilized in the construction and operation of beet factories. Many buildings were made of concrete from his Ideal Cement Company. GW also owned the GW Railroad, linking processing plants to surrounding farms and outside supply and distribution centers. Shown here is one of many "beet dumps" where growers transferred their harvest from wagons to railcars.

Trains pulled by steam engines like the No. 75 were the workhorses of GW's operations from 1907 until 1965. This handsome locomotive became something of a film star in its later years. Engine 75 was featured in movie and television productions including *Breakheart Pass* and *Centennial*, the miniseries based on James Michener's fictionalized history of Colorado.

Great Western Sugar Factory Model

[PLEASE RETURN MAP TO BIN WHEN FINISHED]

N

HIGH DUMPS

BEET SHEDS

COAL STORAGE

SUGAR WAREHOUSES

MAIN BUILDING

BOILER HOUSE

STEFFENS & LIME HOUSE

LIME ROCK

PULP SILO

BLACKSMITH SHOP

GARAGE

FEED YARD

CULTIVATED LANDS

TOOL HOUSE

A scale model of the facility, created by Allen J. Campbell using 1921 blueprints and historical photographs, is part of the Great Western Sugar exhibit at the Loveland Museum/Gallery. The model depicts more than 25 structures, including circular metal storage bins, the boiler house, the packaging and bagging plant, centrifuges, drying beds, lime kilns, beet scales, railroad-related structures, and the administration building.

GREAT WESTERN SUGAR CO.
LOVELAND, COLO.

The processing end of GW's production employed many skilled workers, including chemists. Turning beets into sugar was smelly, unpleasant work. The factory initially employed 800, working 12-hour shifts for 20¢ an hour. During peak harvest times, the factory operated around the clock, befouling clear skies with noxious smoke and putrid steam. But the bad smell that wafted into town seemed a small price to pay for steady prosperity.

GW factories produced granulated white sugar, brown sugar, and powdered sugar for domestic and commercial baking. Beet pulp was used in feed for livestock. Potash, another byproduct of sugar processing, was sold for fertilizer. Some factories, like the nearby Johnstown plant, manufactured the flavor-enhancing chemical MSG.

Sugar beets were relative latecomers on the northern Front Range agricultural scene. The Empson factory opened in 1908 and canned locally grown peas, beans, tomatoes, and cherries. The factory, which sold out to Kuner in 1927, was the first in Loveland to employ women on its production lines. Youngsters riding bikes behind delivery trucks were sometimes lucky enough to gather up fresh produce that bounced off when the trucks crossed the railroad tracks.

Cherry orchards were first planted in the area in the 1870s and helped fuel Loveland's economy in the early 1900s, producing superior fruit year after year. Seasonal workers like these, on David Warnock's farm in 1906, were recruited to hand pick the luscious produce in mid-to-late summer. The demand for delicious Loveland cherry pies and cherry cider spread through word-of-mouth, and their well-deserved reputation grew. Most cherry orchards were west of town, where roadside stands offered everything cherry to locals and tourists alike. By the 1920s, Spring Glade Orchard was the largest cherry grower west of the Mississippi River and seven local canneries were producing $50,000 worth of cherry products a day. Though cherries were unquestionably big in Loveland's economy, they were never quite as big as the ones in the novelty postcard below.

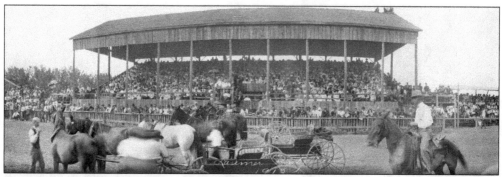

In 1911, the Larimer County Fair spun off from the earlier Corn Roast Festival as an annual August showcase for local agricultural products and livestock. Exhibits of flowers, baked goods, home arts, and textiles filled the fairgrounds buildings. An auto show and machinery displays encouraged visitors to dream big, and a midway featured games of skill and chance. The four-day hoopla eventually included horseracing, a rodeo, and grandstand seating.

Rodeo competitors demonstrated skills at the fair based on the daily challenges of real-life cowboys. For ranch hands, like these branding cattle at the Neville Ranch in 1910, busting broncos and bulldogging calves was all in a day's work.

LUCILLE BELMONT

THE UNDISPUTED WORLD'S CHAMPION AERONAUT. ONLY LADY MAKING A TRIPLE PARACHUTE DROP, THE MOST THRILLING DEMONSTRATION OF THE KIND EVER ATTEMPTED. EVERY DAY AT THE FAIR.

Special stunt shows by barnstormers and balloonists thrilled county fair crowds with feats of derring-do. At the fifth annual event in 1916, lady aeronaut Lucille Belmont wowed onlookers with her trademark triple parachute drop. The big midway ran games and carnival rides day and night. That year's fair promised to present "the biggest and best Amusements, Racing, and Exhibits ever assembled at any Larimer County Fair."

The next big thing in transportation was previewed at the 1910 Corn Roast Festival. Lovelanders of all ages gawked at the cutting-edge contraption, never imagining how dramatically air travel would one day transform tourism in the Rocky Mountains. In 1923, the Gates Flying Circus performed at the festival, stunt flying and dropping copies of their sponsor's *Reporter-Herald* newspaper, some of which included free plane ride tickets, on the enthusiastic spectators.

MRS. THOMAS H. JOHNSON
LOVELAND

Came to Colorado a bride, 1869. Helped to found the Public Library, and was one of the first women elected to a School Board. Member of Currents Events Club and vitally interested in educational matters.

DR. MARY N. KEELER
LOVELAND

An osteopathic physician; Superintendent of the Methodist Sunday School, Secretary of the Board of Education, member of the P. E. O., D. A. R., and the Woman's Club.

MRS. JOHN H. SIMPSON
LOVELAND

Enthusiastic public-spirited worker. Keenly alive to the interests of Church, W. C. T. U., Club, Civic, D. A. R., and other work of the day, helping to organize, and doing state work as well as local.

MRS. M. ALBERTA SPRAGUE
LOVELAND

An active and enthusiastic student of home economics to which subject she gives much of her time and attention. She is a member of the Current Events Club of Loveland.

Representative Women of Colorado, published in 1914, featured portraits of women "who have attained prominence in the social, political, professional, pioneer and club life of the State." Eight Loveland ladies, including these four, were lauded for their service to the community. Dr. Mary Keeler (later Foster, top right) became the first female physician in the area when she moved to Loveland in 1904. She was also a founding member of Chapter L of the P.E.O. Sisterhood in 1905. Eliza Johnson (top left) organized the Women's Professional Club, Elsie Mae Simpson (lower left) was active in Loveland's chapter of the DAR, and Alberta Sprague (lower right) belonged to the Current Events Club. (Courtesy of Brown Palace Hotel Archives.)

Women's clubs, leveraging their combined influence to campaign for cultural improvements throughout the early 1900s, found an unexpected ally in eastern industrialist Andrew Carnegie. The steel tycoon donated millions to build public libraries across the nation. Assisted by Carnegie's largess, Loveland opened its beautiful Carnegie Library in 1908. Children crept down an exterior stone staircase on one side of the building to directly access their own special basement section.

Progressive Era reformers also crusaded for better public education. The 1881 Washington Elementary School burned down and was replaced by this fine brick building in 1905. Proud students and teachers gathered on the school grounds for this postcard picture around 1910. The town's second public elementary school, Lincoln, opened in 1907 at Lincoln Avenue and Fourteenth Street.

Those who excelled in elementary studies and aspired to higher education initially attended classes in the elementary school buildings. Shown above is the Loveland High School graduating class of 1915, with each student numbered for identification purposes. At a time when most Americans' formal education ended with the eighth grade, higher education was a rare privilege. Loveland's burgeoning population soon called for a separate high school facility for its secondary students. The impressive edifice below, the first Loveland High School (now Bill Reed Middle School), was erected on Fourth Street in 1917. Some Loveland graduates of the day went on to attend Colorado Agricultural College (now Colorado State University) in Fort Collins or the University of Colorado in Boulder.

In addition to their studies, high school students played competitive sports. Seen here in fine fighting form is the 1910 Loveland High football team. LHS basketball and baseball teams also competed with other area high schools, with the conviction that athletic competition built both physical strength and character.

Loveland residential neighborhoods proliferated as the town prospered around the turn of the last century. Hundreds of trees were planted along the dusty streets and grassy lawns were watered by irrigation systems and city waterworks. Along with more modest clapboard houses, substantial brick and stone homes like these along Fifth Street were erected by Loveland's prominent upper-middle class citizens.

Transportation innovations and other inventions rapidly transformed everyday life. Newfangled "horseless carriages" like this Loveland mail truck whisked people around the ever-expanding community with speed and efficiency previously unheard of. The increasing popularity of automobiles led to a call for paved streets, drivers' licenses, and traffic regulations. Within a few short decades, auto mechanics would effectively replace the formerly indispensable blacksmith.

Loveland's downtown Rialto Theatre opened in 1919 as part of the local vaudeville circuit. A rollicking variety show featuring singers, dancers, acrobats, and comedians cost 25¢. When moving pictures and "talkies" came into vogue, the Rialto was transformed into a movie house. After struggling through the Depression, the venue thrived anew in 1935 under the management of Ted and Mabel Thompson.

Winter weather along Colorado's Front Range was generally mild, but occasional blizzards were exceptions to the rule. Loveland was hit by a record-breaking snowstorm in 1920, and residents labored to shovel the business and residential districts out from five feet of snow accumulated in less than three days. Hardy Lovelanders made the most of the harrowing blizzard by turning wreckage into recreation. The surprising photograph above proves that at least one resident resolved to put the best possible face on the situation. The creative outdoorsmen below created this 11-man "bobsled" from an old ladder. Jug Riley manned the helm as the crew set out along Lincoln Avenue, south of the Presbyterian Church.

By the 1970s, the sugar beet industry's fortunes were reversing. Concerns grew over environmental pollution from the manufacturing plants, and the beet industry faced competition from less expensive cane sugar. Disputes between labor and the growers led to higher production costs, and GW suffered from low profits and low morale through multiple management changes. Finally, the Colorado beet sugar industry went into a tailspin in the 1970s and never recovered. In 1985, the Loveland factory ceased operations. The GW site, which once stood many miles from the center of town, saw the encroachment of residential and retail development. The dilapidated administration building seen here still stands. Most of the other structures, many made of corrugated metal, rusted and collapsed. For those who remember the factory's glory days and its role in Loveland history, it is a sad sight. (Both, author's collection.)

Four

GATEWAY TO THE ROCKIES

The 1915 opening of Rocky Mountain National Park (RMNP) coincided with the early automobile age. Travelers heading up Big Thompson Canyon to Estes Park and RMNP made Loveland, a few miles east of the canyon mouth, their "Gateway to the Rockies." Here families enjoy camping with tents in the mountains.

British travel writer Isabella Bird, who passed through Loveland en route to Estes Park in the summer of 1873, reported, "These new settlements are utterly revolting . . . with coarse speech, coarse food, coarse everything." Bird boarded briefly with the William Alexander family on future Sylvan Dale Ranch land. She hated the black flies and the rattlesnakes, but found the air both invigorating and conducive to restful sleep. (Courtesy of T. Noel.)

Bird was not the only intrepid lady traveler enticed by the adventure of the wild Rockies. These two dauntless women share a horse on an early 1900s postcard. By the early 20th century, women were pushing the Victorian-era envelope like never before, sometimes setting out on adventures unescorted.

Automobiles offered much more freedom and flexibility than railroad travel. Throughout the 1910s, as this assemblage of vehicles at the Loveland Depot shows, more and more travelers opted for the exciting new individual form of transportation.

AUTO CAMPING PARK, LOVELAND, COLO.

The popularity of motor travel prompted Loveland to establish a free auto camping park at the east end of Fourth Street in the early 1900s, where travelers could pause to refresh before heading for the hills.

In the early days of motoring, roads left much to be desired. Unpaved and rough at best, they became treacherous as they snaked into the mountains. In this 1910s postcard, motorists navigate the sharp turn around Sheep's Head Rock in the Big Thompson Canyon. As the number of auto travelers increased, so did the demand for better roads. The roadbed was shored up with a rock wall winding alongside the river.

Travelers less inclined to rough it in the auto camp found the latest amenities in the Lovelander Hotel at Fourth and Railroad Streets. In 1927, the Elks purchased the building, which they still own. By 1922, the streets in Loveland's business district were paved.

Daley's Barber Shop offered travelers 25¢ baths to wash away the road dust. The "electric lunch" advertised next door to the barbershop at 116 East Fourth Street owed a great debt to Lee J. Kelim, who steam-generated the first electricity for the Big Thompson Milling and Elevator Company in 1900. Five years later, he installed a coal-fired power plant to provide electricity for all the downtown businesses.

Substantial structures of brick and stone along Fourth Street gave downtown a respectable appearance by the early 1900s. The Masonic Lodge building is seen on the left, one of several fraternal organizations that were well established in Loveland by that time. The International Order of Odd Fellows (IOOF) appeared in 1880, followed in 1883 by the Masonic Order.

A large percentage of progressive ladies made up this contingent of the Loveland Current Events Club, ready to head up the canyon to Estes Park in the early 1900s. Prominent local ladies such as Nettie Waite Brandt and Lena B. Gifford served as early presidents of the club, which was dedicated to self-improvement through reading, lectures, and travel. As they campaigned for

national women's suffrage, they considered it their duty as citizens to stay well informed on issues and events of the day, particularly those relating to home, family, and education. Other early women's organizations in Loveland included Eastern Star, established in 1895; the Rebekkah Lodge, founded in 1897; and the Women's Professional Club, organized in 1880.

Decked out in the latest motoring gear, these three independent ladies represent the dauntless women determined to set their own course, without gentlemen escorts. Up the canyon they went, enjoying each other's company as much as the mountain scenery.

Motoring could be an adventuresome pastime for whole families. Here, the Milo Osborn family poses "Fording" the river in their Model T around 1920. (Courtesy of S. Osborn.)

Big Thompson Canyon and the mountains attracted not only scenery buffs, but also outdoor recreationists. Fishing drew sportsmen from the late 1800s onwards. Though not native to Colorado waterways, brown and rainbow trout were prized by both locals and visiting anglers. Here Frend Neville and his fellow fishermen display an impressive string of fish pulled from the Big Thompson in the vicinity of Sylvan Dale Ranch.

Big game also attracted hunters to the Loveland area. This trophy elk, bagged in 1938 by legendary local lady Vena Apgar Snyder, dressed out at more than 1,000 pounds. When she was not hunting, Snyder worked for the Loveland-Estes Park Auto Stage Company, picking up tourists at the depot and driving them up to the park in Stanley Steamers for 12 years. A frequent passenger was F.O. Stanley himself, the inventor of the Steamer.

Early motorists heading up the canyon to Estes Park found welcome respite at many inns along the road. At cozy cabin lodges like this one, travelers could get a bite to eat or even spend the night before continuing on their way into the wilderness.

Mother's Inn, pictured here in the 1930s, offered down-home dining along with a healthy dose of guilt for fibbers on the "Liar's Bench" out front.

Serial Westerns in the early days of cinema sparked America's romance with cowboy culture. Some Loveland area ranchers capitalized on the craze by offering guests a chance to sample the Western experience for themselves. In the 1920s, local cattleman and apple grower Frend Neville built the Sylvan Dale Lodge and four cabins for adventurous guests and sportsmen along the banks of the Big Thompson. (Courtesy of S. Jessup.)

In 1946, Maurice and Mayme Jessup acquired Sylvan Dale with a vision of what the ranch could become. When early television Westerns further fueled the horse-opera hoopla in the 1950s, the dude ranch industry was born. Perfectly positioned to capitalize on this new branch of hospitality, the Jessups and their children, David and Susan, worked hard to enlarge the 125-acre property into a 5,000-acre working ranch with cattle, horses, and guest facilities. (Courtesy of S. Jessup.)

Guests at Sylvan Dale Ranch indulged their inner cowboy/cowgirl with horseback riding, chuck wagon suppers, and square dancing, shown here in the 1950s. The Jessups' tractor-pulled hayrides up the old canyon road were also a popular family adventure. (Courtesy of S. Jessup.)

Today, Sylvan Dale continues to provide a nostalgic retreat from modern stresses. Still family-owned and operated by Susan Jessup and her husband, David Armstrong, the ranch invites guests to saddle up and unwind in a tranquil riverside setting. Modern "dudes" bunk in comfy cabins named for Annie Oakley, Molly Brown, and other Western legends. (Courtesy of S. Jessup.)

The landmark Dude Corral motel and restaurant, owned by Ted and Mabel Thompson, opened in 1947 to welcome Rockies-bound motorists on Highway 34 along the southwestern shore of Lake Loveland. Travelers could eat, rest, and fuel up for the mountain journey ahead. Motorists scarcely had to leave the highway to find a room for the night.

East of town, another iconic travelers' way station opened in 1952. Joe S. Johnson's Corner was in the middle of nowhere along Highway 87 until the construction of the Valley Highway (now Interstate 25) in the early 1960s brought the world to his doorstep. The quintessential truck stop provided food, lodging, and gas for professional drivers and tourists 24 hours a day, 365 days a year. (Courtesy of C. Taylor.)

Johnson's Corner is famous for its great service and massive cinnamon rolls. It was featured in the 1996 Bill Murray film *Larger than Life*. In 2003, the WB2 network named it one of the best roadside attractions in America, and the Food Network named it the "Top Truck Stop Restaurant" in 2004. (Courtesy of C. Taylor.)

Five

WATER DIVERSION HUB

Since the days of the earliest settlers, getting water where it is needed has been an ongoing challenge along the northern Front Range. In 1938, qualified property owners in the Northern Colorado Water Conservancy District, headquartered in Loveland, approved a major diversion project in a special election. The Colorado–Big Thompson Project created a series of reservoirs that enabled more land than ever to flourish agriculturally.

Years before the Big Thompson Project, Loveland's best-known reservoir was created by expanding and flooding the site of a watering hole where David Barnes had rounded up his cattle. Local laborers built a dyke and excavated the area using only shovels and plow-horses. The 1932 Greeley-Loveland Irrigation Company storage basin soon became known as Lake Loveland. Gradually, the community spread northwards to the then-isolated lake, now the scenic centerpiece of town. The new lake nurtured cherry and other fruit orchards along its shores. With the Rocky Mountains in the background, Lake Loveland was picture-perfect, as these and countless other postcards attest.

Lake Loveland and Divide, Loveland, Colo.

Lake Loveland was a boon to local agriculture and a popular recreational spot. From the 1940s through the 1960s, noisy speedboat races buzzed around its waters and water skiers cooled off and showed off at the same time.

This Colorado–Big Thompson Project topographical relief map was built by the Bureau of Reclamation in 1943 and moved to the Loveland Museum in 1952. The huge model gives visitors a bird's eye view of the 2,000-square-mile project, from the western slope to the eastern plains. The map's key includes towns, lakes, reservoirs, waterways, and power plants—more than 125 features in all— including Lake Loveland, in the center.

69

The ambitious water diversion project began with the construction of Granby Dam and Reservoir to collect water from the north fork of the Colorado River on the western slope. From there, the water was lifted 190 feet by three massive electric pumps into Shadow Mountain Reservoir and Grand Lake, seen here on the project relief map. The water then flowed through a mountain tunnel destined for the eastern plains.

Construction of the Alva Adams Tunnel under the Continental Divide was ongoing from 1940 to 1947. When bores from the western and eastern sides met in the bowels of the mountain, they were only one-sixth of an inch out of perfect alignment. The tunnel's eastern portal is 108 feet lower than the western portal, allowing gravity to move the water through all 13.1 miles. This diagram accompanies the relief map exhibit at the museum.

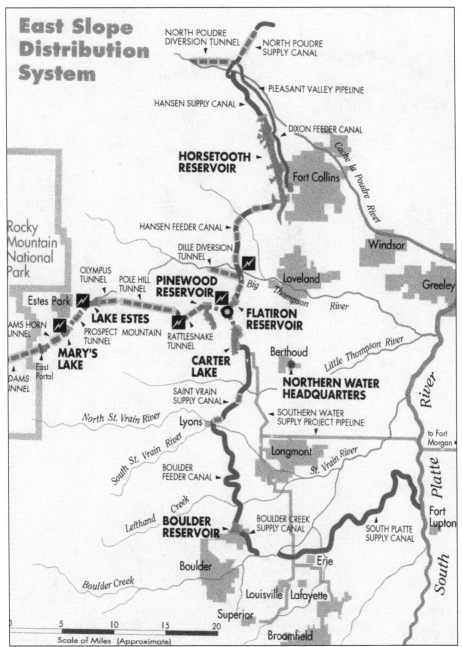

East Slope Distribution System

NORTH POUDRE DIVERSION TUNNEL
NORTH POUDRE SUPPLY CANAL
PLEASANT VALLEY PIPELINE
HANSEN SUPPLY CANAL ▶
DIXON FEEDER CANAL
HORSETOOTH RESERVOIR
Fort Collins
Cache la Poudre River
Rocky Mountain National Park
HANSEN FEEDER CANAL ▶
DILLE DIVERSION TUNNEL
Windsor
OLYMPUS TUNNEL
POLE HILL TUNNEL
PINEWOOD RESERVOIR
Big
Loveland
Greeley
Estes Park
Thompson
River
AMS HORN UNNEL
LAKE ESTES
PROSPECT MOUNTAIN TUNNEL
RATTLESNAKE TUNNEL
FLATIRON RESERVOIR
MARY'S LAKE
DAMS UNNEL
East Portal
CARTER LAKE
Berthoud
Little Thompson River
NORTHERN WATER HEADQUARTERS
SAINT VRAIN SUPPLY CANAL ▶
SOUTHERN WATER SUPPLY PROJECT PIPELINE
North St. Vrain River
Lyons
River
to Fort Morgan
South St. Vrain River
Longmont
St. Vrain River
BOULDER FEEDER CANAL ▶
Creek
Platte
Fort Lupton
Lefthand
BOULDER RESERVOIR
BOULDER CREEK SUPPLY CANAL
SOUTH PLATTE SUPPLY CANAL
Boulder
Erie
South
Boulder Creek
Louisville Lafayette
Superior
Broomfield

0   5   10   15   20
Scale of Miles (Approximate)

This map shows the complex distribution system carrying water to reservoirs, hydroelectric plants, ranches, and farms along the northern Front Range. Rivers, canals, and pipes run north and south of the Big Thompson to storage facilities including Horsetooth Reservoir, Carter Lake, Boulder Reservoir, and Pinewood Reservoir (previously Rattlesnake Reservoir). The project's 12 storage lakes, with a combined surface area of 14,960 acres, have a total storage capacity of 984,975 acre-feet, enough to irrigate nearly 700,000 acres of farmland. The visionary project was completed in 1955 and still supplies the ever-growing Colorado piedmont with both water and electrical power. Recreational opportunities associated with the larger reservoirs are an added benefit for boaters, fishermen, campers, and hikers. (Courtesy of Northern Colorado Water Conservancy District.)

In 1894, one of the first water management projects along the Big Thompson River, the so-called Big Dam, was completed near the mouth of the canyon by stonemason Charles Lester, engineer John H. Nelson, and contractor George Kelly. The remarkable stone and concrete arch-type dam replaced an 1880 log dam. The Loveland water supply came from the Big Dam via filter plants to the southeast.

The Dam Store and Chasteen Park just below the Big Dam were popular stops for sightseers along the old road to Estes Park. The first Dam Store dated back to 1910. Rome and Ombra Dietrich ran an upgraded mercantile in that same location until 1935, when Highway 34 bypassed their location.

In 1935, Highway 34 was built to the south, bypassing the Big Dam. The structure at the mouth of the canyon along the highway has always been known as the Little Dam. This later version of the Dam Store, run by Ted and Mabel Thompson, peddled souvenirs from postcards to "fool's gold." The big pipe over the highway was part of the Colorado–Big Thompson Project.

All four sons of the pioneering Osborn family posed in their field for this photograph. Llewellyn Osborn (far right) served as Loveland's city engineer from 1919 to 1941. Among his many contributions was his design of the domestic waterworks, including a cement storage tank on a hill west of town. The tank was a graffiti magnet for decades, with every high school class trying to overwrite previous classes with new spray-painting on the landmark. (Courtesy of S. Osborn.)

With a civil engineering and irrigation degree from Colorado A&M, Lew Osborn was also instrumental in launching the Municipal Light and Power Plant in Big Thompson Canyon. The city purchased the land from Mariano Medina's stepson, Louis Papa (left) in 1926. The streamside park provided a lovely picnic area just up the canyon, but Charles Viestenz had another vision for it. With his election to the Loveland City Council in 1911, Viestenz led a campaign to construct a hydroelectric power plant for the city. After 13 years, he saw his dream realized when the plant began operations in Viestens-Smith Park in February 1925.

The Osborn estate donated a lot where the family home once stood at Fifth Street and Lincoln Avenue for Loveland's first museum in 1938. An unimpressive building from the outside, the Pioneer Museum was akin to a treasure chest in a plain brown wrapper. Cobbler, collector, and chronicler of local history Harold Marion Dunning contributed his own assemblage of pioneer and Indian artifacts to establish the museum's first real collection on January 1, 1946. Both Dunning and his son, Harold Bell Dunning, spent countless hours cataloging and labeling the historical items. Dunning Sr. resented not being given the credit he felt due, wanting "at least a bronze marker on the building in some very conspicuous place, crediting Harold M. Dunning with the founding of the museum."

Local business owner and history buff Rome Dietrich was another avid collector of Indian artifacts who donated many of his acquisitions to the new museum. Dietrich is seen here surrounded by mounted displays of arrowheads and spear tips, Indian baskets, pottery, and weavings.

Like most old museums, Loveland's was a veritable "cabinet of curiosities." For the most part, artifacts were displayed willy-nilly, arranged out of context and telling a jumbled story of the past at best. Nevertheless, "home folks," newcomers, tourists, and schoolchildren tromped through the place wide-eyed for decades, gleaning what they could about Loveland's earliest inhabitants, first settlers, geology, and wildlife from the mounted historical objects.

The Colorado–Big Thompson Project was one of many New Deal programs intended to get people back to work during the Great Depression. The city of Loveland also added two major edifices in the 1930s with New Deal funding. The Pulliam Building, which became known as the Community Building, was erected on Cleveland Avenue in 1939. It housed city hall as well as one of the largest civic auditoriums in the area. Loveland's Cadman Music Club, established in 1925 by Opal Glasgow, sponsored concerts and musicals and purchased a grand piano for the building. Namesake David T. Pulliam owned several farms and was the director of the Consolidated Home Supply Ditch Company. He donated the site, as well as $28,000 for the building. (Both, courtesy of Denver Public Library Western History Collection.)

The post office on Cleveland Avenue was completed in 1937, with its main lobby featuring a dramatic pioneer mural by Works Projects Administration (WPA) artist Russell Sherman. New Deal funding also paid for the paving of every downtown alleyway. All the streets in town were black-topped by 1940.

Throughout the Great Depression and World War II, Loveland survived, thanks to initiatives like the Colorado–Big Thompson Project. A four-block downtown along Fourth Street bustled with dress shops and shoe stores, furniture and hardware stores, drugstores, and haberdasheries. Loveland managed well in those lean years, but would truly flourish in the optimistic postwar 1950s.

Six

SWEETHEART CITY

Though the town's name did not come from romantic inspiration, postmaster Elmer Ivers thought Loveland could capitalize on the popular misconception. He consulted Ted Thompson, president of the chamber of commerce, and together they came up with an idea that still characterizes the community today. Ivers is seen here with Margaret Davidson, Miss Loveland Valentine of 1967, who showed him what she thought of the idea.

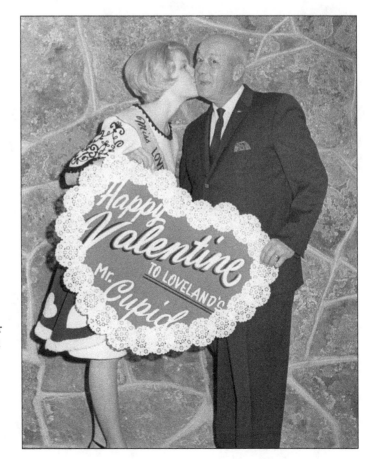

Ivers's idea was to create a special program where people would mail their valentines to Loveland to receive the very appropriate postmark on the envelope. The postal department cooperated by issuing a special cancellation stamp. Before long, valentines came pouring into the post office, and in 1947, the first re-mailing program was officially launched.

The program gained nationwide exposure in 1950 when Guy Lombardo featured the song "There's a Lovely Lake in Loveland" on his radio show on Valentine's Day. In response, Ed Garrett, a Loveland businessman, named Lombardo honorary mayor of Loveland. That year, 12,000 valentines arrived for re-mailing. Seen here are the silhouettes of horseback riders along lovely Lake Loveland's shores in 1948. (Courtesy of Denver Public Library Western History Collection.)

It quickly became apparent that the post office staff could not handle the crush of valentines by themselves. Fortunately, there were plenty of volunteers happy to spread the warm-hearted spirit of Loveland. Getting together to stamp the valentines became a much-sought-after pastime. For 10 days before Valentine's Day, over 60 volunteers still spend four to five hours a day hand-stamping each heartfelt missive. A different local eatery sends in free lunch each day.

As the success of the re-mailing program continued, a mascot was added to the fun, and Loveland's Cowboy Cupid was born. He wore a cowboy hat, chaps, boots, and a great big smile. A local lad was lassoed into the job each year. Here, Timmy Gibson was overwhelmed with valentines in 1961.

A Valentine's Day Remembrance
Is a very gracious way
Of showing those you care for most
They're thought about today.

So let the memories fill your heart
And let the day be bright
For knowing you has been to me
A time of pure delight.

T.W.T.

The inevitable next step was to create an annual official Loveland valentine. In 1964, a call went out to the community for inspired assistance. For many years, Ted Thompson composed the inside verses and local artists contributed the designs. The emphasis was always on love, happiness, beauty, and of course the town of Loveland.

The cover of this 2009 valentine illustrates another Valentine's Day custom. Lovelanders were invited to buy a red wooden heart from the Rotary Club and write a brief valentine message for public display. The various hearts were then posted on light poles throughout the city. The proceeds from the heart cutouts go to a local charity selected by the Rotarians each year.

It's here
Valentine Cachet for 1960

It's fun to be remembered
On this very special day

When Cupid's brand on Valentines,
True words of love convey.

—Loveland, Colorado

Another addition to the Loveland valentine re-mailing program was a cachet stamped on the outside of each envelope. The verse was chosen from a local competition; this one appeared on the 1960 valentine. It could be stamped in either red or black ink, depending on the envelope color. The Cowboy Cupid cachet told the recipient right away that there was something special inside.

Cowboy Cupid ambassadors selected from local elementary schools promoted the valentine program for decades. Here, little Billy McCreary and Ann Gregg pose outside the post office in 1958.

POST OFFICE

MAIL A VALENTINE VIA *Sweetheart Town* LOVELAND COLO.

1958
Bill McCreery

The children seen mailing valentines on the cover of this book attended Garfield, Loveland's newest elementary school, built at Colorado Avenue and Eighth Street in 1950. The single-story building featured three wings of classrooms. For years, the new school dominated the annual inter-elementary track meets, outperforming its archrivals, who were derided as "Lincoln Stinkin'," "Washington Washtub," and "Big T Broken Knee." (Courtesy of Denver Public Library Western History Collection.)

Early Cowboy Cupid Kenny Eicher had the right idea for spreading the valentine spirit far and wide. Valentine cards addressed to the Loveland postmaster for re-mailing arrived from countries around the world, usually via airmail.

Beginning in 1961, Miss Loveland Valentine was selected from a group of high school senior girls to represent the re-mailing program and Loveland. Several candidates were nominated by classmates and interviewed by members of the chamber of commerce. The lucky girl chosen spoke to the Colorado legislature in Denver and presented the governor with a box of valentine candy. Carol Johnson, Miss Valentine 1979, is seen here with Governor Richard Lamm.

Miss Valentine 1975 Sandy Shideler (far right) poses with the other girls of her "court." They are, from left to right, Pat Morris, Sherrianne Bruce, Cindy Smith, Beki Benson, and Chris Buehler. Though only Sandy was privileged to wear the special Miss Valentine outfit, all of the girls promoted the re-mailing program through personal appearances and interviews. (Courtesy of B. Ballam.)

Representing the valentine program was time-consuming work, but there was still time for fun. The 1966 contenders for Miss Valentine were, from left to right, Mary Chrisman, Marcia Fawcett, Laree Kiely, Cindy Shelton, and Mardi McCreary. In 1984, 2003, and 2007, the US post office gave a boost to the re-mailing by issuing "LOVE" postage stamps.

Ted and Mabel Thompson, shown here with Rome Dietrich, were the chaperones for Miss Valentine for many years. They accompanied her to all her presentations and speeches and especially her trip to the state capitol in Denver. The Thompsons kept her on schedule and were always there to handle any last-minute emergencies.

February weather permitting, a hot-air balloon rally added a colorful lift to the annual Valentine's Day celebration beginning in the 1980s. People still come from miles around to watch the balloons float above the Sweetheart City. (Courtesy of Engaging Loveland.)

Loveland Chamber of Commerce boosters have long supported local events such as the valentine re-mailing. The Whiskerinos sported beards for the 1959 centennial of the "Rush to the Rockies" by gold prospectors. Their female counterparts, the Bustle-ettes, sported enhancements on the posterior side. Later known as the Booster Club and the Red Coats, chamber promoters gave speeches, designed signs, and wrote newspaper copy touting the virtues and desirability of Colorado's Sweetheart City.

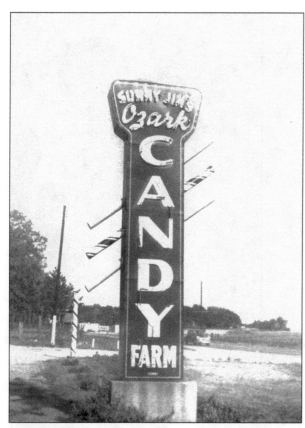

Romance and chocolates have long gone together, and Sunny Jim's Candy Farm, located west of Loveland on the way to Estes Park, concocted superb valentine chocolates every year, including those presented to the governor. Jim and Edna Walters came to Loveland in 1963 from Missouri, where their candy business had been almost too successful. They hoped to semi-retire here, taking several months off after every Valentine's Day. But in spite of their efforts to cut back, the excellence of their candy made it one of the most popular spots in Loveland. (Both, courtesy of E. Walters.)

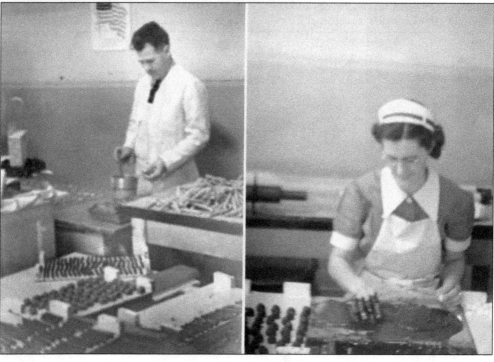

Other Loveland businesses positioned themselves along Highway 34 going into the canyon. In 1933, the Proctor family moved to Loveland and discovered the beautiful veined pink alabaster in Owl Canyon. Earl Proctor began carving different decorative articles from the distinctive stone and giving them to friends. The ashtrays, bowls, bookends, and salt-and-pepper shakers he made became so popular he was urged to make more for sale. His daughters, Madge, Hazel, and Gladys, soon got involved, and the business thrived for 40 years, eventually managed by Hazel and Gladys.

HOME of MRS. BENSON'S CIDERS

Take cherry orchards, an entrepreneurial spirit, and roadside stands between Loveland and the mouth of the Big Thompson Canyon and you have the makings of a successful business. Nellie Benson began selling chilled cherry juice and cider to locals and tourists in 1925 and her home and cherry cider stand, shown here on a 1950s postcard, endured for decades as a refreshing oasis for mountain-bound motorists.

Leland Huston opened the Rocky Mountain Pottery Company in 1957 and his unique products were a hit. Some pieces had a bark-like finish infused with pine scent, while glazed items featured hand-painted twigs of evergreen with pinecones. Such quaint cottage industries contributed more to the local charm than they did to the Loveland economy and as the 1950s drew to a close, community leaders began to cast about for bigger commercial fish.

Seven

HIGH-TECH PIONEER

One of the most successful
electronics companies of the
latter 20th century started with a
humble yet revolutionary oscillator.
Inventor Bill Hewlett (pictured)
teamed up with former Stanford
classmate Dave Packard to
manufacture the low-cost precision
instrument and incorporated in
1947. Over the ensuing decades, the
company grew into an international
enterprise. In 1959, Loveland
narrowly edged out Boulder in
the competition for Hewlett
Packard's first manufacturing
plant outside of Silicon Valley.
(Courtesy of K. Jessen.)

This Model 200A audio oscillator was the first of many cutting-edge HP products. Disney's chief sound engineer on *Fantasia* was their first customer, and the company prospered as pioneers in the electronics industry, ultimately producing everything from optical components to printed circuit assemblies. By the company's 15th anniversary, it had 700 employees and monthly sales topping $1 million, and the founders began looking to expand. (Courtesy of K. Jessen.)

A coin toss determined whether Hewlett (left) or Packard (right) would lead the name, and the company itself. Packard's family ties to Pueblo made Colorado a natural choice for HP's expansion. Loveland businessmen Paul Rice and Bob Hipps spearheaded an effort to jumpstart the stagnated local economy by developing a major industrial park to attract manufacturers. Their entreaties impressed the founders and HP announced plans to make Loveland its second home. (Courtesy of K. Jessen.)

HP set up its first temporary facility in the former Handy Glass building (above) on Lincoln Avenue, training new employees for wiring and assembly jobs. They soon constructed the first building of their own at Third Street South and Lincoln Avenue (below). The Interim Plant, also known as the Components Building, opened in June 1960. An old Quonset hut on Lincoln Avenue housed the first research and development (R&D) group in Loveland. (Both, courtesy of K. Jessen.)

This architect's drawing of the proposed Hewlett Packard campus to be erected in Thompson Valley Industrial Park, southwest of town on Fourteenth Street, envisioned three buildings to be constructed consecutively as the operation grew. Work on Building A commenced in the fall of 1961. The sprawling facility incorporated space not only for three assembly lines of production, but also for R&D, personnel, purchasing, order processing, and shipping. Building B opened in

May 1966 to accommodate more production, warehousing, offices, conference rooms, and an employee cafeteria. Before the cafeteria, Stan Williams, the owner of Wayside Inn in Berthoud, brought a hot food wagon on site at lunch and dinner times, so it was only natural that Williams became HP's first cafeteria manager. By 1971, HP's Loveland division employed more than 1,700 people. (Courtesy of Denver Public Library Western History Collection.)

The October 13, 1962, grand opening of HP's Building A was a milestone event for the community. Seen here playing up the Western locale of the new facility are early managers Joe Barr, Marco Negeste, Dan Cullen, and Stan Selby. As Loveland's first district manager, Selby modeled "The HP Way" of empowering employees to determine their own strategies to meet management's objectives. (Courtesy of K. Jessen.)

Along with the local Jaycees, Hewlett-Packard was a sponsor of Loveland's first Soap Box Derby in 1963. The gravity-powered cars rolled along Fourteenth Street and down the hill upon which HP was perched. A few years later, the racetrack moved to West Twelfth Street, east of Taft Avenue. Here, racer Doug Benson, sponsored by the Home State Bank, flashes a confident victory sign before the heated competition in August 1967. (Courtesy of D. Benson.)

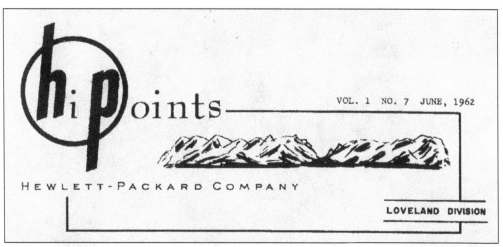

HP's in-house publication *Hi Points* was the voice of the Loveland division. Started as a saddle-stitched booklet in December 1961, it evolved into a magazine printed on coated stock by January 1966. The first editor, Kay Therp, included both personal and corporate developments in *Hi Points*, keeping every employee in the loop month after month. Each department contributed content, while features covered employee engagements, marriages, babies, and significant milestones. (Courtesy of Hewlett Packard.)

Hi Points cartoonist Jerry Farm lightened up the sometimes snooze-inducing content with illustrations like this one of an engineer at work. Regular features of the publication included company sports coverage, service awards, introductions of new employees and new products, and even a "Poet's Corner." *Hi Points* contributed significantly to the sense of workplace family, which Hewlett and Packard considered so important to the company culture. (Courtesy of Hewlett Packard.)

HP threw its first Loveland Division picnic at Sylvan Dale Ranch in September 1960 for 36 employees. Hewlett and Packard themselves helped to prepare and serve the food, getting casually acquainted with their Loveland crew in the process. As the company grew, so did the annual event. In August 1963, the company purchased and opened Highland Park, a recreational facility off Highway 34. The bigger and better picnics included pony rides, clowns, and games for kids, like the popular Penny Hunt. Adults enjoyed a shooting gallery with cigarette-pack targets and cigarette prizes. In 1966, the company picnic moved again with the purchase of Hermit Park, about a mile from Estes Park. This facility had electricity, three year-round cabins, and onsite caretakers. (Both, courtesy of K. Jessen.)

From the beginning, Hewlett and Packard characterized their style as "management by walking around." Here Packard greets one of the Loveland division's female assembly-line employees. HP employed many women and was very progressive, hiring women for managerial and engineering positions. Reflective of the times, however, they were referred to as "gals" or "girls" and were paid less for doing the same work as male counterparts. Women were considered better suited to assembly work because of their patience and because their smaller fingers were less clumsy with tiny components. HP designated "Housemothers"—officially titled Administrative Directors of Women—who acted as counselors and ombudsmen, helping female employees cope with workplace problems to raise morale and lower turnover. (Courtesy of K. Jessen.)

Miss December

Susi Moomaw

Escorted by
CHAUNCEY TAYLOR
Sponsored by
L CLUB

Despite a growing feminist awareness and objections to beauty pageants, Loveland High School's annual Calendar Girl contest continued into the 1970s. Young ladies representing the various school clubs paraded in formal dresses and answered poise and personality questions, in the style of the Miss America pageant. Judges selected 13 winners—one for each month, plus a cover girl—to grace the student council's fundraising calendar. (Author's collection.)

As young ladies' hemlines inched ever higher in the 1970s, Loveland High School authorities were impelled to establish a maximum allowable height above the knee for skirts. Girls could not wear pants to school until 1970, when LHS administrators conceded that trousers were acceptable during the three winter months only, in order to keep legs warm. Here, Suzan Yelek (standing) and Debbie Hutchinson see how their hems measure up. (Author's collection.)

Another Loveland High School tradition that endured into the 1970s was Rag Day. Started in 1906 as a protest against "Sunday Best" student dress requirements for visiting school board officials, it evolved into a cherished spring ritual. The rags became costumes for song and dance skits performed in the school gymnasium. By the 1950s, the annual class competition was a major fundraiser for the school athletics "L" Club. The showcase of imaginative skits and musical numbers was featured in a *Denver Post* story in 1960. Pictured here are the senior boys and girls of the class of 1971 hamming it up as prison inmates and suffragists. Sadly, student exuberance and school administration support gradually waned, and Rag Day faded into history in 1984. (Both, author's collection.)

Even as new buildings were going up in Loveland, others were coming down. On September 26, 1973, the spontaneous combustion of volatile grain dust blew the side out of the Big Thompson Mill and Elevator in a massive explosion. Two people were killed and five others were injured in the blast, which also destroyed more than 10,000 pounds of grain. A similar explosion at the Loveland Elevator in 1925 seemingly had failed to inspire safety measures that might have prevented the 1973 accident.

Tourists continued to pass through Loveland on their way to the mountains. This visitors kiosk erected in the 1970s along Highway 34 between the Interstate 25 exit and the east side of town provided information on local motels, restaurants, shopping, and auto services, as well as Loveland events and points of interest. (Courtesy of Denver Public Library Western History Collection.)

Other light industrial firms followed HP's lead and came to the Loveland area throughout the 1960s and 1970s. Among them was Samsonite's Lego factory, manufacturing the snap-together plastic building blocks that still fire young imaginations. The Lego plant closed in 1977. All that remains of the building's original tenant is this public art piece, "Lego My Heart." (Author's collection.)

On the eve of Colorado's 100th birthday, nature gave residents, who were cocksure with water engineering and technological achievements, a lesson in primal supremacy. A thunderstorm stalled over Estes Park and dumped more than 12 inches of rain in less than four hours. As the water raced down the canyon, the steep and narrow channel funneled it into a raging torrent. The Big Thompson rose nearly 20 feet in some places, dragging debris from bridges, fences, and buildings as it rushed downhill. Propane tanks were ripped from their moorings; automobiles were swept from the highway. Many in the canyon who were told to evacuate and climb to higher ground did not take the warning seriously, and 145 people were killed. These photographs show a house along the river (above) and Sylvan Dale Ranch (below) in the aftermath. (Below, courtesy of S. Jessup.)

The July 31, 1976, Big Thompson Flood was the worst natural disaster in the state's history. The death toll was high, despite the heroic efforts of paramedics, firefighters, and other emergency personnel. Loveland Memorial Hospital (shown here) was overwhelmed. Five Monfort feedlots' refrigeration trailers were set up behind the hospital to store bodies and body parts awaiting identification. (Courtesy of Denver Public Library Western History Collection.)

Ominous dark clouds hung over Big Thompson Canyon for two full days after the disaster. In the weeks following, property damage was estimated at $30 million. More than 418 homes and 52 businesses were completely destroyed by the force of the debris-choked water. Great swaths of Highway 34 were washed away, especially near the mouth of the canyon. Huge cranes like this one were brought in to assist with the cleanup. (Courtesy of J. Hemberger.)

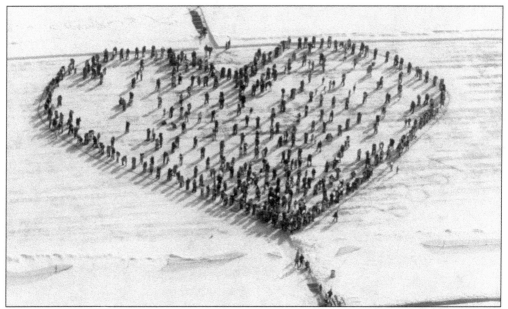

After the flood, life in Loveland eventually returned to normal. The canyon highway was rebuilt, but structures were no longer allowed in the flood zone. Local traditions continued, sometimes with a new twist. Loveland romantics gathered in the shape of an arrow-pierced heart for the first annual Great Loveland Kiss-Off in 1989. Sponsored by the chamber of commerce, the event set a world record for most couples simultaneously smooching.

In a bizarre postscript to Loveland's sugar story, 582,000 gallons of low-grade molasses oozed from a ruptured storage tank on the old GW site in 1990. The spill spread over a half-mile area, creating an obstructive mess along Madison Avenue. The sticky situation called for creative thinking. Someone struck upon the idea of adding lye to the molasses. The resulting chemical reaction crystallized the gooey syrup, and front loaders took it from there.

106

The Fort Collins–Loveland Airport, dedicated northeast of town in 1966, became increasingly important as big corporations moved into the area. Originally used by only private pilots, the airfield has since expanded to accommodate Boeing 727s and 737s flying Allegiant Airlines routes to Las Vegas and Phoenix. The 85,000-foot runway often serves corporate jets as well. Private planes like those above share airport space with air ambulances, firefighting tankers, and flight schools. (Both, author's collection.)

The HP manufacturing facility—the three buildings in the center—closed in the 1990s and was subsequently reborn as Agilent Technologies. In turn, a declining Agilent sold the property to the City of Loveland in June 2011. That same month, the Colorado Association for Manufacturing and Technology (CAMT) announced an ambitious undertaking. In partnership with NASA and the National Renewable Energy Lab (NREL), CAMT proposed an Aerospace Clean Energy (ACE) manufacturing and innovation park. Multiple companies would share the space, transforming NASA, NREL, and university-held patents into products with a fast-tracked marketing schedule. The project is predicted to bring 7,000–10,000 manufacturing, research, and development jobs to the area. This satellite image may presage the facility's future. Should a project like ACE land successfully, it will be one giant leap for Loveland. (Courtesy of GeoEye.)

Eight

SCULPTURE CAPITAL

The first public sculpture in Loveland was a miniature copy of the Statue of Liberty, donated to the city by the Boy Scouts in 1954. Still lifting her lamp on the east side of Lake Loveland, with the mountains in the background, she stands as a welcoming beacon to travelers, not unlike the original Lady Liberty in New York Harbor. (Denver Public Library Western History Collection.)

Artist Peter Toth brought something new to the public art scene when he chose Loveland as the site for one of his wooden Indians. Toth's goal was to carve an Indian from a tree trunk in each state. Loveland received the honor for Colorado, perhaps in part because the high school teams were called the Loveland Indians. In 1979, Toth's "Redman" was installed on the south shore of Lake Loveland. Over the years, the sculpture has been moved to several other locations. It is presently maintained in a field along Highway 34 west of town.

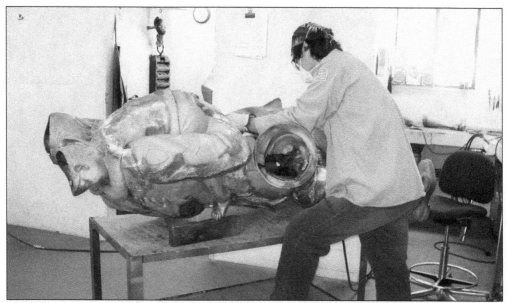

Seven years earlier in 1972, Bob Zimmerman, a metallurgical engineer, had started an industrial foundry making metal parts for manufacturing. His business evolved into Art Castings, which today turns out some 2,500 finished sculptures each year. The convenience and the reputation of the foundry brought many artists to Loveland. In 1985, Art Castings was sold to Richard Gooding and now has 52 employees. Art Castings uses the "lost wax" process, which dates back thousands of years. After the artist creates a sculpture, a mold is made of the original. Then it goes through eight more steps: wax pouring, wax chasing, spruing, ceramic shell, metal pouring, welding, and metal chasing. Finally, using various chemicals, a patina is applied to the finished piece to create subtle color. (Both, author's collection.)

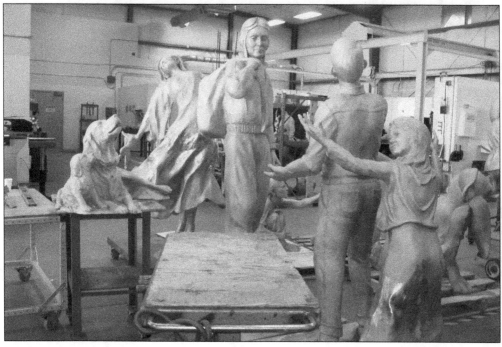

In 1983, local sculptors George Lundeen, Dan Ostermiller, George Walbye, Fritz White, and Hollis Williford developed the idea of a sculpture show providing an outdoor public venue for sculptors to exhibit and sell their work. Their brainchild, Sculpture in the Park, has grown to be America's largest outdoor sculpture showcase event. Pictured here clockwise from upper left on the stairs are artists Ostermiller, Williford, Jay Eighmy, Walbye, White, Ben Iizany, and Gala Knight. Clockwise from upper left on the landing below are Lundeen, Gary Voss, Ronnie Williford, and Lavoy Brown. In 2011, a total of 170 sculptors participated in the show, exhibiting 2,000 pieces of art. The Loveland High Plains Art Council hosts the event and each year purchases sculptures for Benson Park. (Photograph by Blair Godbout, courtesy of G. Walbye.)

The Loveland Sculpture Invitational shares the same August weekend as Sculpture in the Park. Held adjacent to Loveland High School, the Invitational has provided $220,000 for K-12 art education and has donated 20 sculptures to the city. The Thompson Valley Art League's Arts and Crafts Festival is also held that weekend, in North Lake Park. (Author's collection.)

Benson Park, today the single largest showplace of Loveland public sculpture, began on a site donated by the Benson family. In 1877, Aaron Shaw Benson, pictured with his extended family, homesteaded a tract of land in what is now Loveland. Robert Benson purchased the land from his grandfather in 1907 and farmed it for 38 years. In 1961, Robert donated a portion of the land for wetlands and a refuge for birds.

By 2011, Benson Sculpture Garden was home to 130 fine art sculptures. In a variety of styles and media, all are complemented by the landscaping in the garden itself. Shown here are "Great Blue Heron" by Hollis Williford (left) and "Dragonflies in Composition" by Jack Kreutzer. (Both, author's collection.)

A stroll around the sculpture garden reveals a delightful array of characters, including this cowboy, "Between Broncs" by Garland Weeks, and children playing ring-around-the-rosy in "Circle of Peace" by Gary Price. (Both, author's collection.)

By no means limited to the Sculpture Garden, public art permeates the entire community of Loveland. A paperboy loading papers on his bike pauses appropriately outside the *Reporter-Herald* offices in "Home Delivery" by Blair Muhlenstein. A vintage cinematographer sets up his camera in front of the Rialto Theatre with "Persistence of Vision" by Pat Kennedy. (Both, author's collection.)

Jane Dedecker based "Overdue" on an old photograph of the Deal family siblings returning library books in their wagon. Mark Lundeen's "Mighty Casey" prepares to knock one out of the park at the municipal baseball diamonds. These permanent residents in delightful frozen poses enhance the quality of life for all the city's residents and visitors. Loveland was the first city in Colorado to designate one percent of sales revenue for public art acquisitions and installation. (Both, author's collection.)

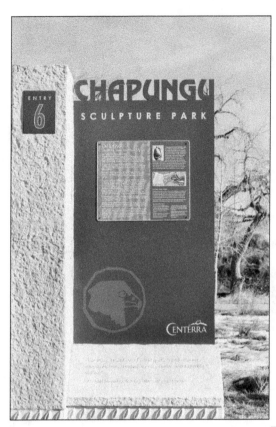

Chapungu Sculpture Park is a far cry—and several miles—from Benson Sculpture Park. Although both display sculpture in a garden setting, their artistic styles are very different. Carved by artists in Zimbabwe, the figures in Chapungu are made of stone rather than cast bronze. In 2006, these unique pieces found their way to Loveland. Chapunga Park, with 26 acres of landscaping and 82 sculptures, is a popular setting for concerts, wine tastings, weddings, and fundraisers. (Both, author's collection.)

The Centerra development, which includes the Chapunga Sculpture Park, is a major commercial center on both sides of Interstate 25 north of Highway 34. Developed by Chad and Troy McWhinney in the 1990s, the complex includes the Pavilions pictured below, the Promenade Shops, and even a skating rink. The design incorporates mountain themes in its highway signs and bridges, and patterns of local agriculture in its award-winning landscape architecture. The Centerra Natural Area uses innovative storm-water guidelines to ensure a rich ecosystem of wetlands and wildlife. In 1989, the McWhinney brothers sought out their great-great-grandfather John Hahn's Colorado property, lured from California by a *Time* magazine article declaring the Front Range of Colorado a "place to watch" for future development. Like Thomas Edison, the McWhinneys believed "success often follows those who get ahead of the inevitable." (Both, author's collection.)

The McWhinneys bought their first acreage from their grandmother and began planning. The Loveland Outlet Center, opened in 1994, was their first project. Since then they have developed many shopping and business complexes, as well as residential enclaves, all incorporating open spaces and parks. The top sign describes the wildlife area maintained by the High Plains Environmental Center near the McWhinneys' office buildings. The McWhinney-Hahn Sculpture Park, located east of town near the Loveland Visitors Center, ties together the past and future of the community. Their great-great-grandfather, John Hahn, would be proud of his descendants' accomplishments and their stewardship of his former ranchlands. (Both, author's collection.)

In 2004, the Larimer County Fair moved from its old site on Loveland's First Street to "The Ranch," a large complex east of Loveland. Other attractions staged throughout the year at the venue include car shows, gun shows, Indian powwows, and motorcycle rallies. The Budweiser Events Center, part of "The Ranch" pictured here, hosts large performances previously seen only in Denver, like the Harlem Globetrotters, *Riverdance*, *Cirque d'Soleil*, and other big-name entertainers. The center is also home to the Colorado Eagles professional hockey team. (Author's collection.)

In a nod to the city's valentine traditions, the heart-shaped sculptures seen around town exist thanks to Engaging Loveland, a program launched by Judy Rethmeier, Susan Davis, and Kim Vecchio in 2007. Artists furnished sketches of their ideas for the hearts to business sponsors, who then selected their favorites. Trying to find all 21 of the hearts around town is a fun challenge. "Small Town, Big Heart" by Ross Lampshire (pictured) adorns the Loveland Visitors Center. (Author's collection.)

Two years after the hearts began popping up, the Loveland Visual Arts Commission challenged Northern Colorado artists to decorate the very necessary but unattractive electrical transformers around town. Enthusiastic painters each submitted a model and a resume in the competition to beautify the boxes. In 2009, a total of 23 transformers were transformed. Over the next two years, 20 more were painted. Pictured here is "Kalila and Dimna: Fables of Bidpal" by Lyse Dzija. (Author's collection.)

A determined contingent of local preservationists battled to save and reconceptualize one of Loveland's most iconic buildings more than a century after it was built. The 1891 Loveland Farmers Milling and Elevator Company—now known as the Loveland Feed and Grain—was once the center of a major local industry but has been abandoned for years. Plans are underway to restore the relic and use it as a workspace and showcase for future Loveland art. Artspace, a Minneapolis-based company, along with Denver-based architects, have purchased an acre of land surrounding the building for residential units where artists and their families can live and work. The mill itself will be used for a studio area and gallery.

The Loveland Museum added an art gallery in 1970 and, in a major 1992 remodel, doubled its size to incorporate three galleries. A re-creation of Mariano Medina's cabin, a model of the sugar beet factory, and a relief map of the Colorado–Big Thompson Project are just a few peeks into the past the museum provides. Changing exhibits, workshops, and lectures on various topics make Loveland history accessible to all.

The purple mountains are majestic, but it was the fruitful plains that sustained early Loveland settlers. Local artist Richard Schilling finds himself drawn to the prosaic prairie time and again. A retired dentist, Schilling divides his time between painting and establishing dental clinics in Third World countries. This painting was part of his exhibition of watercolors and ink sketches at the Museum/Gallery in early 2012.

The functions and forms of Loveland have been various and many since its gold-rush-era inception. Industries and emphases have changed. Priorities have shifted. People have come, people have gone, and more people have made this place their home. But through it all flows the river that first attracted settlers and travelers and that continues to enrich this very special Colorado community.

BIBLIOGRAPHY

Addressing History: The Pioneering Women of Loveland in Period Costume. Loveland, CO: Loveland Museum/Gallery, 2011.

Benson Sculpture Garden. Loveland, CO: W.W. Design, 2009.

Big Thompson Disaster. Loveland, CO: Lithographic Press, 1976.

Dunning, Harold Marion. *Over Hill and Vale.* Boulder, CO: Johnson Publishing Co., 1956.

———. *Over Hill and Vale, Vol. III.* Boulder, CO: Johnson Publishing Co., 1971.

Feneis, Jeff and Cindy. *Exploring Loveland's Hidden Past.* Loveland, CO: Loveland Museum Gallery, 2007.

Gates, Zethyl. *Mariano Medina: Colorado Mountain Man.* Boulder, CO: Johnson Publishing Co., 1981.

Gates, Zethyl and Ann Hilfinger. *Historical Images from the Loveland Museum/Gallery Collection.* Virginia Beach, VA: Donning Co., 1994.

Jessen, Kenneth. *How It All Began: Hewlett Packard's Loveland Facility.* Loveland, CO: J.V. Publications, 1999.

———. *The Great Western Railway.* Loveland, CO: J.V. Publications LLC, 2007.

Loveland–Big Thompson Valley, 1877–1977 Centennial. Loveland, CO: Loveland–Big Thompson Valley Centennial Commission Inc., 1977.

Loveland Publishers and Pioneers. Longmont, CO: Lehman Communications Corp., 2005.

Parrish, Shirley Rietveld. *Epic of Larimer County.* Fort Collins, CO: Win-Art Inc., 1959.

Semple, James Alexander. *Representative Women of Colorado.* Denver: Williamson-Haffner Company, 1914.

INDEX

DISCOVER THOUSANDS OF LOCAL HISTORY BOOKS FEATURING MILLIONS OF VINTAGE IMAGES

Arcadia Publishing, the leading local history publisher in the United States, is committed to making history accessible and meaningful through publishing books that celebrate and preserve the heritage of America's people and places.

Find more books like this at
www.arcadiapublishing.com

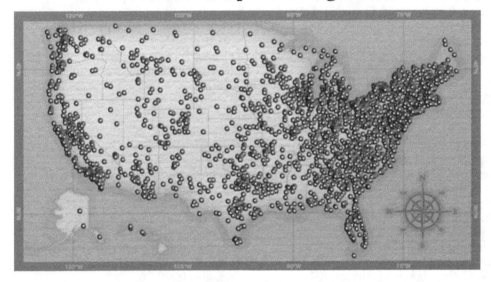

Search for your hometown history, your old stomping grounds, and even your favorite sports team.